Around and About

Our globe, our world

Kate Petty
and Jakki Wood

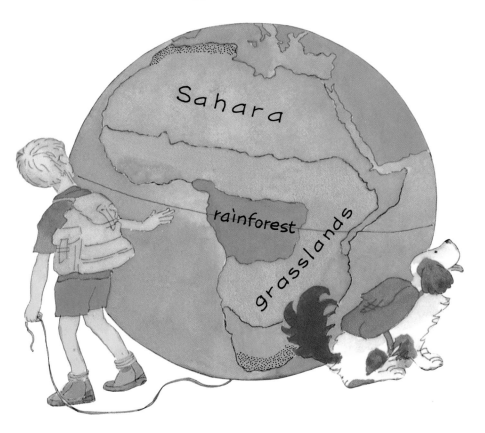

Barron's

First edition for the United States, Canada, and the
Philippines published 1993 by Barron's
Educational Series, Inc.

Designed and produced by
Aladdin Books Ltd
28 Percy Street
London W1P 9FF

All inquiries should be addressed to:
Barron's Educational Series, Inc.
250 Wireless Boulevard
Hauppauge, NY 11788

International Standard Book
No. 0-8120-1236-4

Library of Congress
Catalog Card No. 92-30580

**Library of Congress Cataloging-in-
Publication Data**

Petty, Kate.
Our globe, our world / Kate Petty–1st ed.
p. cm. – (Around and about)
Includes index.
Summary: Harry and Ralph find out about
their world by studying a road map, world map,
and globe while going on a journey on land and
sea.
ISBN 0-8120-1236-4
1. Geography–Juvenile literature. [1. Geography. 2.
Maps.] I. Title. II. Series: Petty, Kate. Around and
about.
G133.P424 1993
910–dc20   92-30580   CIP   AC

Printed in Belgium

3456 4208 987654321

Design David West Children's
Book Design
Illustrator Jakki Wood
Text Kate Petty
Consultants Keith Lye B.A., F.R.S.G.,
Eva Bass Cert. Ed., teacher of
geography to 5-8 year-olds

Contents

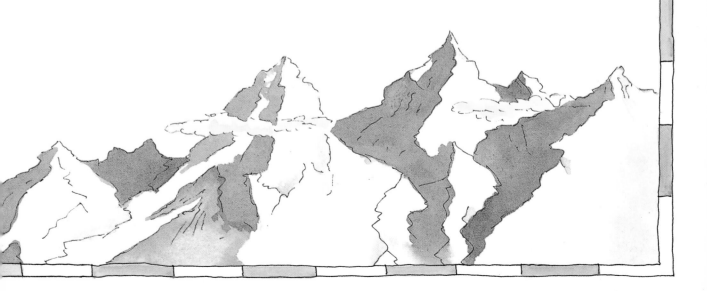

Greetings from Yorville.

Preparing for a journey

Harry and his dog Ralph want to go to the seaside. What is the best way to get there? They look at a map to find out.

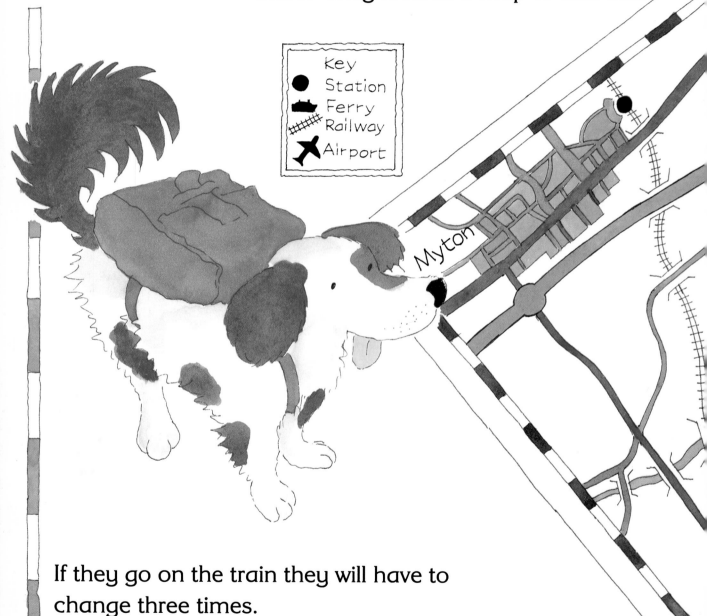

Key
● Station
⬛ Ferry
Railway
✈ Airport

Myton

If they go on the train they will have to change three times.
It's not far enough to go by plane, and anyway there isn't an airport near their town.

By train, we'd have to change at Woodham, Camford and Creek to get from Myton to Yorville.

How would they get there by road?

Road maps

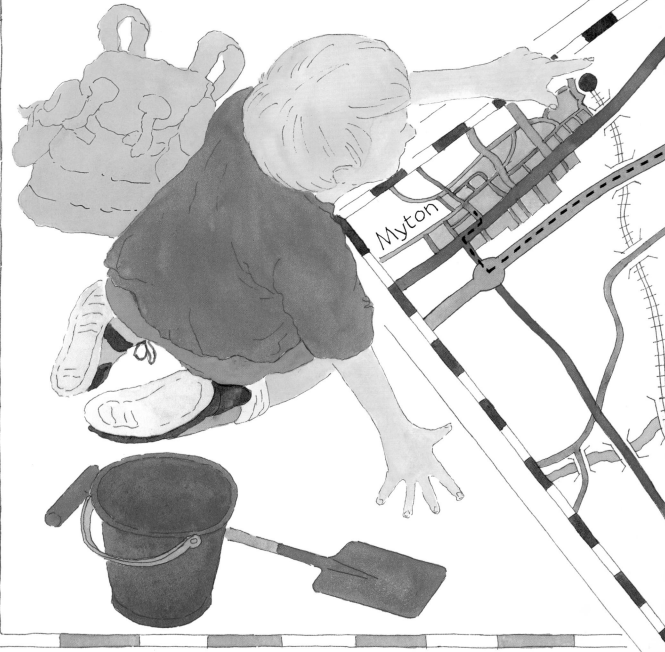

They look closely at the road map. The highways are colored blue. The main roads are colored dark red. Roads colored light red also will be quite fast. Roads colored brown are narrow roads and lanes.

Myton

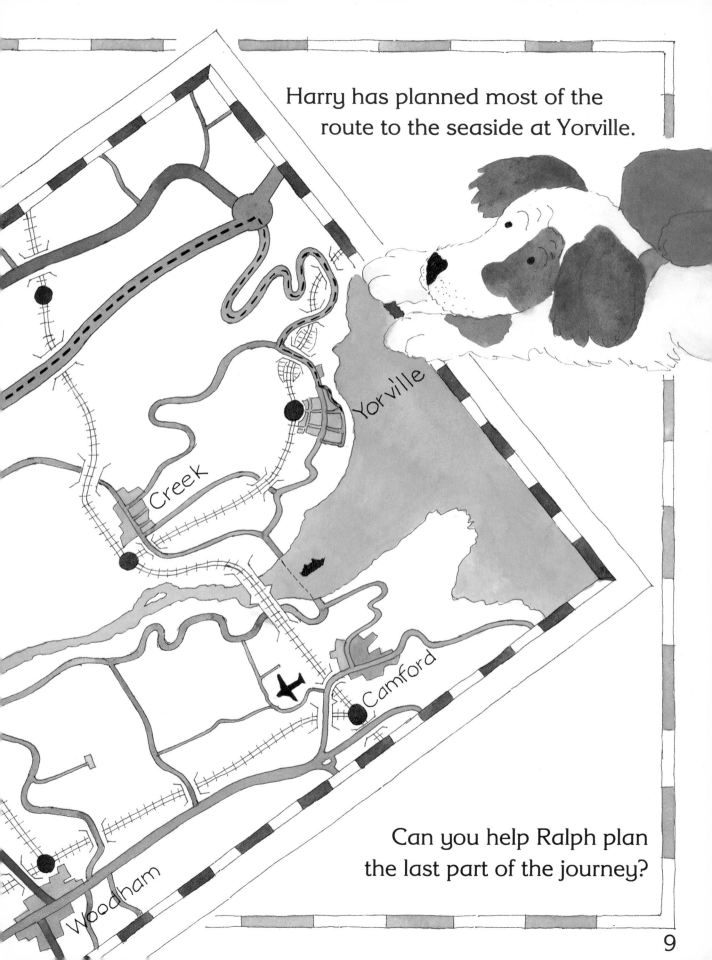

Harry has planned most of the
route to the seaside at Yorville.

Yorville

Creek

Camford

Woodham

Can you help Ralph plan
the last part of the journey?

9

Where the land meets the sea

Here they are at the coast! Harry and Ralph are on the edge of the land where it meets the sea.

Let's go to look at the horizon.

We'll never reach it, but let's go anyway.

They walk along the coast path. When they look into the distance they seem to see the place where the sky meets the sea. This is called the horizon. They can't see any further because the round surface of the planet curves away from them.

Why can't Harry and Ralph visit the horizon?

Crossing water

Harry wants to cross the ocean to the next huge piece of land. You have to cross several oceans if you are going to travel the world. Can you think of some other ways of crossing the ocean? There's no land in sight! Most of the world looks like this. Nearly three-quarters of the planet is covered by water.

Harry and Ralph approach the coast of another country. It's a good thing they have their passports!

They arrive in France – which is on the huge piece of land known as the continent of Europe. They see miles of lush, rich, farmland.

Can you find out which crops grow in Europe?

The globe

Traveling is fun for Harry and Ralph. They look at a map of the world to decide where to go next. It's easy to forget that the world isn't flat, like a map. It's round like the globe.

Harry blows up an inflatable globe.

All that blue is the water! At the top of the globe is the North Pole. The South Pole is at the bottom. An imaginary line drawn around the middle is called the equator.

I can play ball with it!

equator

The equator

Harry wants to find out what it's like at the equator. They look at the globe to see the places on the equator. They decide to visit Brazil in South America. Will they be able to see the line around the equator?

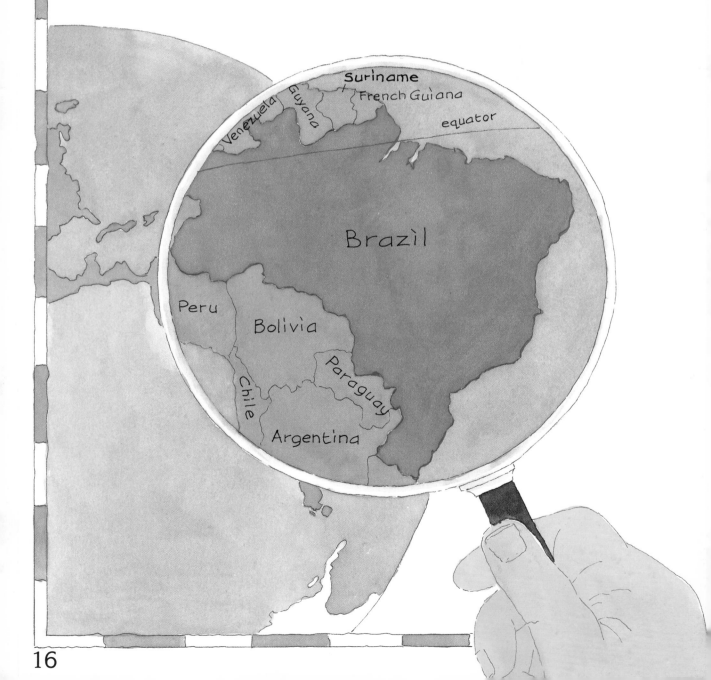

It's hot and steamy at the equator. There are thick rainforests of large plants and tall trees.

The poles

Now Harry and Ralph visit the poles. What's it really like at the poles? It's cold! The North Pole is in the middle of the frozen Arctic Ocean. The Inuit people live in the northern lands, close to the North Pole. Polar bears and other animals that live there need to have very thick fur.

Asia

Russia

Siberia

North Pole

Europe

Arctic Ocean

Greenland

Alaska

Canada

U.S.A

Arctic Ocean

North Pole

Greenland Pole

The South Pole is in the middle of a frozen continent called Antarctica. It is the coldest place in the world.

Penguins are some of the few creatures that can survive here.

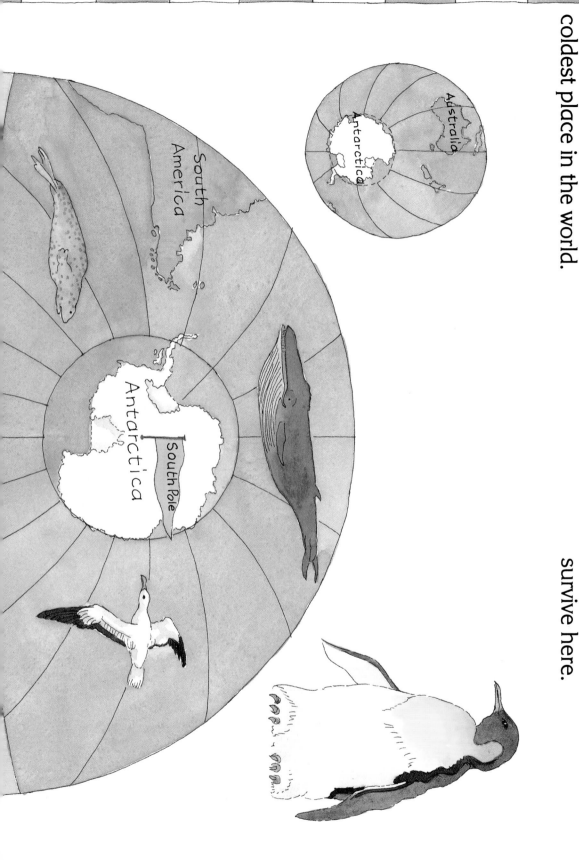

Desert and grasslands

Ralph can't wait to fly off to the hottest place in the world. That's the Sahara – a desert on the continent of Africa. They look at the globe. The Sahara desert spreads across several African countries. Can you see which ones they are? There is hot sun, but little rain. It's very hard to grow things.

Between the desert and the rainforest of Africa there are flat, grassy plains. Lions and zebra roam among these grasslands.

The highest mountain

Harry and Ralph have visited the hottest and the coldest places in the world. They have seen deserts and ice, rainforest and grassland.

Now Harry wants to find the highest mountain. Mount Everest is 29,028 feet (8,848 meters) high. It is part of a 1,550 mile (2,500 km) range called the Himalayas.

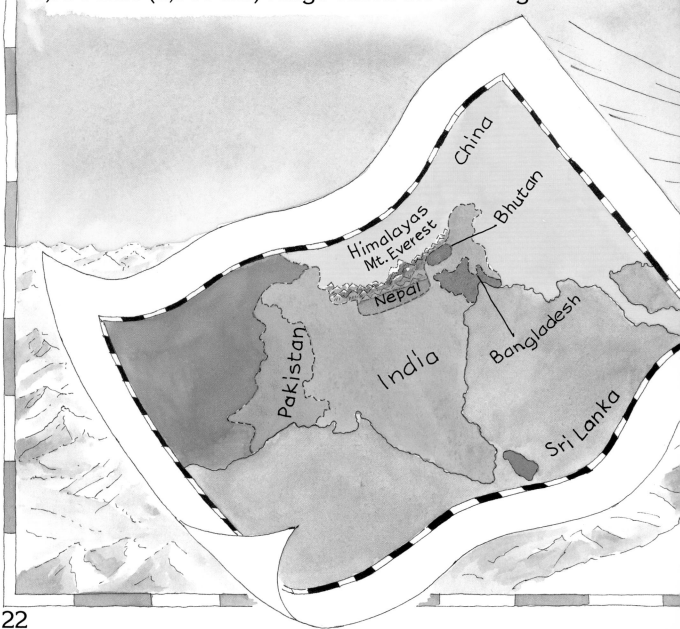

Harry and Ralph can see the mountains marked on the map in the continent of Asia. Mount Everest is on the border between China and Nepal.

The continents

Look at the seven different-colored groups of countries on this map of the world. Each one is a continent. What are they called? Which ones have Harry and Ralph visited?

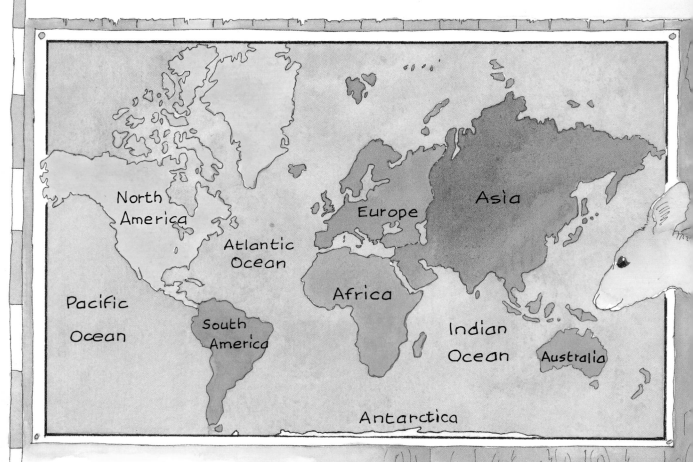

France is a country on the continent of Europe. The United States and Canada are countries on the continent of North America. But Australia is a country that is also a continent!

Can you name these Australian animals?

The countries of the world

This map shows most of the countries of the world. There are about 200 of them so there isn't enough room to label every single one.

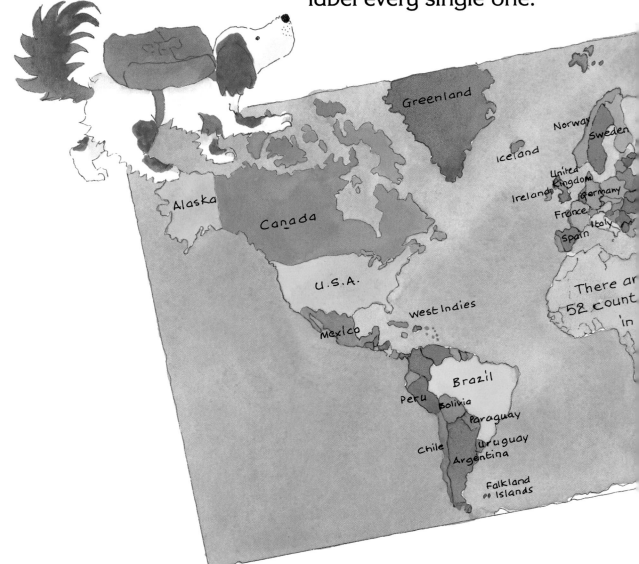

Greenland

Norway

Sweden

Iceland

United Kingdom

Ireland

Germany

France

Italy

Spain

Alaska

Canada

U.S.A.

West Indies

Mexico

There ar
52 count
in

Brazil

Peru

Bolivia

Paraguay

Chile

Uruguay

Argentina

Falkland Islands

Find the biggest countries.
Find your country.
Compare them for size.

Harry looks at maps and books to find out more facts about the different countries. See how many books about the countries of the world you can find.

Canada is a bit bigger than China, but there are forty times as many people in China.

Biggest:
1. Russia
2. Canada
3. China
4. United States
5. Brazil
6. Australia

Smallest:
1. Vatican City
2. Monaco

Sakubona 你好嗎 صباح الخير مرحبا

People of the world

Maps and globes can tell you a lot about the countries of the world but they can't tell you much about the people who live there.

Harry and Ralph are trying to find out how people from other countries live and what languages they speak. They have made a questionnaire. Harry has filled in one about Ralph. Now he's filling in one for himself.

Language: English
Home: brick house
Transport: bike, hot air balloon
Favorite food: french fries pizza

Language: barking
Home: kennel
Transport: hot air balloon
Favorite food: bones

You can look at books and pictures about different countries and fill in questionnaires about the children who live there.

Index

This index will help you to find some of the important words in the book.